Literary Elements

ELEMENTS OF
Literature
FIRST COURSE

TRANSPARENCIES
WORKSHEETS
TEACHING NOTES
ANSWER KEY

D1224296

HOLT, RINEHART AND WINSTON
Harcourt Brace & Company

Austin • New York • Orlando • Atlanta • San Francisco • Boston • Dallas • Toronto • London

STAFF CREDITS

Associate Director: Mescal Evler
Manager of Editorial Operations: Robert R. Hoyt
Managing Editor: Bill Wahlgren
Project Editor: Katie Vignery
Component Editors: Victoria Moreland, Colleen Hobbs
Editorial Staff: *Associate Editors,* Kathryn Rogers, Christopher LeCluyse; *Assistant Managing Editors,* Amanda F. Beard, Marie H. Price; *Copyediting Supervisor,* Michael Neibergall; *Senior Copyeditor,* Mary Malone; *Copyeditors,* Joel Bourgeois, Gabrielle Field, Suzi A. Hunn, Jane Kominek, Millicent Ondras, Theresa Reding, Désirée Reid, Kathleen Scheiner; *Editorial Coordinators,* Robert Littlefield, Mark Holland, Jill O'Neal, Marcus Johnson, Tracy DeMont; *Assistant Editorial Coordinator,* Summer Del Monte; *Support Staff,* Lori De La Garza, Pat Stover, Matthew Villalobos; *Word Processors,* Ruth Hooker, Margaret Sanchez, Kelly Keeley, Elizabeth Butler
Permissions: Tamara A. Blanken, Ann B. Farrar
Design: *Art Director, Book Design,* Richard Metzger; *Art Director, Book & Media Design,* Joe Melomo
Prepress Production: Beth Prevelige, Simira Davis, Sergio Durante
Media Production: *Production Manager,* Kim A. Scott; *Production Coordinator,* Belinda Barbosa; *Production Supervisor,* Nancy Hargis
Manufacturing Coordinator: Michael Roche

ISBN 0-03-053242-6

1 2 3 4 5 6 7   27   02 01 00 99

**LITERARY ELEMENTS
TRANSPARENCIES AND WORKSHEETS**

CONTENTS

ABOUT THE LITERARY ELEMENTS TRANSPARENCIES AND WORKSHEETS

The transparencies, teaching notes, and worksheets in the *Literary Elements* booklet for the *Elements of Literature* series provide opportunities to broaden students' knowledge and appreciation of literature and poetry. This booklet contains teaching materials that support specific selections and features in the Pupil's Edition. The following are some of the benefits of using these *Literary Elements* materials:

- They provide an alternative method of teaching and expanding on the various Pupil's Edition selections and features.
- They are designed to address the needs of students with diverse learning styles and educational needs, including advanced and slower-paced students, as well as independent and group learners.

Literary Elements Transparencies focus on a specific literary element that is presented in an Elements of Literature feature and a corresponding literary selection from the Pupil's Edition. These transparencies offer students practice and reinforcement in identifying literary terms and techniques.

Literary Elements Teaching Notes support the transparencies and contain the following features:

- *Presentation* offers suggestions for presenting the material, including activities for extending the lesson.

- *Alternative Uses of the Transparency* suggests other contexts in which students can use the teaching strategies and the transparency.
- *Transparency Answer Key* provides possible responses to questions and activities on the transparency.

Literary Elements Worksheets build on the lesson presented in the transparencies and teaching notes and offer students further practice on specific literary selections and Elements of Literature features. A Worksheet Answer Key follows the Literary Elements Transparencies and Worksheets section of the booklet.

When used together, the transparencies, teaching notes, and worksheets form a comprehensive lesson that amplifies and supports instruction on literary elements presented in the selections and Elements of Literature features in the Pupil's Edition.

Collection One   Out Here on My Own

THE ELEMENTS OF A SHORT STORY

RIKKI-TIKKI-TAVI

TEACHING NOTES

This material is designed to be used with "Rikki-tikki-tavi" (Pupil's Edition, page 3) and with the feature Elements of Literature: The Short Story: A Story's Building Blocks (Pupil's Edition, page 22) in Collection One. In this lesson, students will identify the elements of a short story.

Presentation

1. After students have read "Rikki-tikki-tavi" and the Elements of Literature feature, place The Elements of a Short Story transparency on the overhead projector and ask volunteers to define the elements.

2. Divide the class into six groups. Have each group fill in the element boxes on a copy of the transparency or on their own paper with answers appropriate for "Rikki-tikki-tavi."

3. When the groups have finished, ask group representatives to come up to the overhead projector, one at a time, to fill in one of the element boxes in the diagram.

4. You may wish to ask students for other possible answers. Point out that students may have different opinions concerning the major elements of the story. For example, some students may think that the main conflict is internal (Rikki-tikki's struggle to prove himself) rather than external (Rikki-tikki's struggle with the cobras Nag and Nagaina).

5. As an extension activity for students, have them imagine how "Rikki-tikki-tavi" would be different if it were written from the point of view of Nag and Nagaina. Have students write a short summary of this version of the story. Then, have them draw and complete a diagram of the story's elements, showing the conflicts, the complications, the climax, the resolution, and the theme. When students have finished, ask volunteers to read their summaries aloud and to explain their diagrams. Point out that a story retold from a new perspective may seem different.

    Ask students whether they are more sympathetic toward the snakes in their revised versions than in the original, and why or why not. If necessary, explain that students may identify more with the snakes in their own versions because these revisions make the snakes more familiar to the reader. They may also sympathize more with Nag and Nagaina because the snakes have concrete things to fight for and defend—their home and children—while Rikki-tikki kills the snakes because they are a traditional enemy.

6. As an alternative extension activity, divide the class into groups. Tell students to think of a personal conflict they feel comfortable sharing or a situation in a story or television show in which someone faces a conflict. Have each student freewrite a short paragraph describing the conflict, the complications, the climax, and the final resolution. When students have finished, have them read their paragraphs aloud to the group or exchange papers. Then, have them tell one another what they liked best about the writings.

Further Practice

For further practice on elements of a short story in "Rikki-tikki-tavi," give students the worksheet on page 4.

Alternative Uses of the Transparency

Students can use copies of the transparency to develop their own stories. You can use the transparency with any other short story.

TRANSPARENCY ANSWER KEY

Basic Situation and Conflict: Rikki-tikki and the cobras Nag and Nagaina are natural enemies. Rikki-tikki confronts them when he comes to live with Teddy and his parents.

Complications: Nag plans to kill Teddy's father; Rikki confronts Karait; the cobra eggs are ready to hatch; Nagaina threatens Teddy.

Climax: Rikki-tikki's fight with Nagaina

Resolution: Rikki-tikki is praised for ridding the garden of the snakes and saving the family. He finally accepts his place at the table, eating his fill of the family's food.

Characters: Rikki-tikki-tavi, Darzee the tailorbird, Chuchundra the muskrat, Teddy and his mother and father, Nag and Nagaina the cobras, and Karait the small snake

Theme: Everyone has his or her own natural strengths and abilities. We will be successful and accepted as long as we use those abilities and strengths to benefit our families and communities and not for our own personal advantage.

ELEMENTS OF LITERATURE   FIRST COURSE   **LITERARY ELEMENTS**

Collection One   Out Here on My Own   **WORKSHEET 1**

Rikki-Tikki-Tavi, PUPIL'S EDITION PAGE 3
Rudyard Kipling

Discovering Elements of a Short Story

A **short story** is a brief fictional prose narrative. It is usually built on a **plot,** or series of related events, that include several elements. The **basic situation** (or **exposition**) provides information about setting and background. The **conflict** is a struggle between opposing characters or forces; it is intensified by further **complications.** The **climax,** the turning point of the story, is the moment of the story's highest emotional intensity, when the outcome of the conflict is made clear. During the **resolution,** the complications of the plot are finally tied together.

Understanding Elements of a Short Story

Answer the following questions on "Rikki-tikki-tavi" on the lines provided.

1. What is the main conflict in the story?

_____

2. What complication follows the killing of Nag?

_____

3. What is the climax of the story?

_____

4. What is the story's resolution?

_____

Applying Skills

5. Usually, a short story has at least one main character who wins the sympathy of the reader. This character keeps the reader turning pages to find out what will happen to him or her. As the title implies, Rikki-tikki-tavi is the star of this story. At what points in the story do you find yourself sympathizing with him? Explain why you feel as you do. Write your answer on a separate sheet of paper.

RECOGNIZING TONE IN NONFICTION

from HOMESICK

TEACHING NOTES

This material is designed to be used with the excerpt from "Homesick" (Pupil's Edition, page 105) and the feature Elements of Literature: Nonfiction: Encountering Our Lives (Pupil's Edition, page 121) in Collection Two. In this lesson, students will identify and summarize the elements of tone in "Homesick."

Presentation

1. After students have read the selection and the Elements of Literature feature, begin the discussion by asking students to look up the word *tone* in a dictionary. The following questions will guide the discussion:
   - Which of the definitions of the word *tone* applies to an element of literature, such as the way an author tells about an incident? *A manner of expression showing a certain attitude.*
   - If a reporter were writing about an automobile accident, for instance, would her tone be subjective or objective? *Objective.*
   - Would the reporter be likely to include her opinions and feelings about the accident? Why or why not? *No. The reporter's job is to report the facts and let readers draw their own conclusions.*
   - What kinds of writing might be subjective, or include the writer's opinions and feelings? *Essays and autobiographies.*

2. Place the Recognizing Tone in Nonfiction transparency on the overhead projector. Ask students to identify phrases or incidents from the selection; write student responses in the appropriate spaces on the transparency.

3. As an extension activity, have students think of incidents from their own lives. Have each student compose a paragraph about a particular incident, writing as an objective reporter. Then, have students include their feelings that they are willing to share as they write about the same incident in a second paragraph. Ask volunteers to read their paragraphs to the class.

Further Practice

For further practice on tone in "Homesick," give students the worksheet on page 7.

Alternative Uses of the Transparency

You can use the transparency with other essays in Collection Two and with articles from newspapers or magazines to reinforce students' skills in identifying the elements of a writer's tone.

TRANSPARENCY ANSWER KEY

Subjective

1. The writer is a displaced American who feels she is not really American because she doesn't live in the United States.

2. The writer feels as though she doesn't belong where she lives, but that she could never really be an American because she could never be president of the United States.

3. The writer tells about refusing to sing the British national anthem because she felt she would be disloyal to America if she did, and she recounts her fear when Ian Forbes tried to force her to say "God Save the King." The writer also tells about feeling small in the hall of the house and about becoming angry because she had to learn things from her friend Andrea. Her descriptions of her classmates, the servants, and the beggars reveal her personal feelings.

Objective

1. Students might say that the brief descriptions of the wall around the house, the Chinese words on a page, Mud Flats, and the information about how the city was divided into sections are objective.

2. The writer is objective only briefly when describing her surroundings in China. She quickly moves to her own story.

   The tone of this selection is subjective because the writer includes her emotions and feelings as she discusses each incident.

ELEMENTS OF LITERATURE FIRST COURSE **LITERARY ELEMENTS**

Collection Two   Who Am I?

WORKSHEET **2**

from HOMESICK, PUPIL'S EDITION PAGE 105
Jean Fritz

Discovering Tone in Nonfiction

Like the tone of a person's voice, the **tone** of a work of nonfiction gives the listener or reader a sense of the speaker's attitude toward the subject. Tone is conveyed through the writer's choice of words and details. A factual piece, without emotion or opinions, is considered **objective** in tone. A piece in which the author explains how he or she feels, gives a private opinion, or reveals a personal response to a situation is **subjective** in tone.

Understanding Tone in Nonfiction

For each of the following excerpts from "Homesick," decide whether the excerpt is objective or subjective. On the line provided, write **O** for objective and **S** for subjective.

_____ **1.** "And I was on the wrong side of the globe." (page 105)

_____ **2.** "Our house stood behind a high stone wall, which had chips of broken glass sticking up from the top to keep thieves away." (page 107)

_____ **3.** "The Russian and German concessions had been officially returned to China, but the people still called them concessions." (page 111)

_____ **4.** "He was tall and mysterious-looking, more like a character in my *Arabian Nights* book than a man you expected to talk to." (page 112)

Applying Skills

5. By the end of the story, the reader is familiar enough with the narrator's life that the reader understands her emotions even when the writing is more factual than emotional. What do her final two actions—correcting her fake English lesson to Lin Nai-Nai and facing Ian Forbes—tell us about the narrator's mood at the end? Why does she feel this way? Write your answer on the lines below.

_____

_____

_____

_____

_____

_____

ANALYZING POINT OF VIEW IN A STORY

AFTER TWENTY YEARS

TEACHING NOTES

This material is designed to be used with "After Twenty Years" (Pupil's Edition, page 193) and the feature Elements of Literature: Point of View: Through Whose Eyes? (Pupil's Edition, page 202) in Collection Three. In this lesson, students will analyze point of view.

Presentation

1. After students have read the selection and the Elements of Literature feature, place the Analyzing Point of View in a Story transparency on the overhead projector. Review the concept of point of view. Discuss the differences between first-person, third-person limited, and omniscient points of view. Answer questions students may have.

2. Use the following questions to begin the discussion of "After Twenty Years":
   • Who is the narrator? *The narrator is an unseen observer of the action.*
   • What does the narrator tell you about the characters? Does the narrator tell you what the characters think? How do you get most of your information about the characters? *The narrator describes the actions and appearances of the two characters. The narrator also explains what is described, but does not tell what the characters think. Readers get most of their information about the characters through dialogue, with the remainder coming from description, explanation, and opinion.*
   • Does the narrator have a more favorable opinion of Jimmy than of Bob? Explain. *The only clues to the narrator's opinion of the two characters are in the descriptions of both. The narrator describes Jimmy as impressive and confident. The narrator describes Bob's show of wealth as being "enlarged by success." Thus, students might argue that the narrator's opinion of Jimmy is more favorable overall than his opinion of Bob.*

3. Have students answer the questions on the transparency. When they are finished, ask them from which point of view "After Twenty Years" is told. If necessary, explain that the story is told from the omniscient point of view.

4. As an extension activity, have students rewrite the story from Jimmy Wells's point of view. Tell them that they may use either the first-person or third-person limited point of view in their stories.

5. As an enrichment activity, have students write a paragraph in the first-person point of view about a decision they once made. Then, have them exchange paragraphs with a partner and rewrite their partners' paragraphs, using the omniscient point of view. Ask students to compare their feelings toward their original paragraphs with those they have toward their partners' rewrites. Make sure that students write about incidents that they are willing to share.

Further Practice

For further practice on point of view in "After Twenty Years," give students the worksheet on page 10.

Alternative Uses of the Transparency

You can use the transparency with novels and other stories.

TRANSPARENCY ANSWER KEY

First-Person Point of View

1. I (possibly we).

2. A character in the story.

3. Narrator can only describe what he or she sees, knows, and thinks.

Third-Person Limited Point of View

1. He or she (possibly they).

2. Unseen observer not in the story.

3. Narrator describes only what one character in the story sees, knows, and thinks.

Omniscient Point of View

1. He or she (possibly they).

2. Unseen observer not in the story.

3. Narrator can describe what any of the characters in the story sees, knows, and thinks. Narrator can give information unknown to the characters and can express an opinion about the characters and the story.

LITERARY ELEMENTS

Collection Three   Do the Right Thing

WORKSHEET **3**

AFTER TWENTY YEARS, PUPIL'S EDITION PAGE 193
O. Henry

Discovering Point of View in a Story

Every short story has a **point of view,** or the position from which the story is told. Point of view can be **omniscient,** with an all-knowing narrator; **first person,** told by an "I" who tells only his or her own thoughts and observations; or **third-person limited,** with an outside narrator revealing the thoughts and observations of only one character ("he" or "she").

Understanding Point of View in a Story

Answer the following questions about point of view in "After Twenty Years" on the lines provided.

1. From what point of view is "After Twenty Years" told?

_____

2. What information is withheld from the reader in the first scene, in which Bob talks with a policeman?

_____

3. What information is withheld when the second man comes along and listens to Bob's reminiscences?

_____

4. How would the portrayal of Bob's personality have been different if the story were told from another point of view?

_____

Applying Skills

5. The author's choices of what not to tell give this story its impact. Why would the ending be weaker if the story had been told from inside Bob's head, revealing his feelings? Write your answer on a separate sheet of paper.

Collection Four   We Rookies Have to Stick Together   TEACHING NOTES **4**

THE ELEMENTS OF DRAMA   BRIAN'S SONG

TEACHING NOTES

This material is designed to be used with *Brian's Song* (Pupil's Edition, page 274) and with the feature Elements of Literature: Drama: An Introduction (Pupil's Edition, page 270) in Collection Four. In this lesson, students will identify the dramatic elements in *Brian's Song*.

Presentation

1. After students have read the teleplay and the Elements of Literature feature, review the Elements of Literature feature, and then place The Elements of Drama transparency on the overhead projector. Use the following items to focus the discussion:
   - Brian Piccolo and Gale Sayers are football players. A football game shares many of the elements of drama. Describe how a drama and a football game are alike. *A football game is similar to a drama because there are players, who are equivalent to the cast of characters in a drama. One football team could be seen as the protagonist, and the other as the antagonist. External conflict occurs as each team tries to win the game. Internal conflict occurs within individual players as they compete with the other players or themselves. Complications arise as one team gets the ball or defends its territory. Climactic endings may occur in football games with exciting final touchdowns or close scores. Resolution occurs when one team wins the game.*
   - What other sports or games share the elements of drama? *All competitive sports share the elements of drama. Some examples are soccer, hockey, tennis, baseball, basketball, skiing, swimming, and track.*

2. Pair students with partners they do not usually work with. Using the transparency, have each pair identify and discuss the dramatic elements of *Brian's Song*. Ask students to identify the most important dramatic element in this teleplay and to explain their answers. *Responses may vary. Some students may argue that the protagonists are the most important element; others may feel that the conflicts the protagonists experience are the most important.*

3. As an extension activity, have students write a short paragraph comparing their own experiences of working with unfamiliar people to Brian and Gale's experience of working with each other.

4. As another extension activity, you may ask students to choose a sport that they enjoy either as participants or as spectators and to describe that particular sport to a partner as if it were a drama. To make sure students include all of the elements of drama in their descriptions, you might hand out copies of the Elements of Drama transparency. You may also choose to have students write their descriptions.

Further Practice

For further practice on elements of drama in *Brian's Song*, give students the worksheet on page 13.

Alternative Uses of the Transparency

Students can use copies of the transparency when they evaluate a movie, play, or dramatic television show. You can also use the transparency when students write original plays.

TRANSPARENCY ANSWER KEY

Characters: Gale Sayers, Brian Piccolo, Coach George Halas, Linda Sayers, Joy Piccolo, various Chicago Bears coaches and players, doctors, nurses

Protagonist(s): Brian, Gale

Antagonists(s): Brian, Gale, Brian's cancer

Exposition: In 1965, Gale and Brian compete as rookies on the Chicago Bears professional football team.

Conflict(s): Brian and Gale's friendly rivalry while trying to get on the team; their rivalry for the same position; Brian's conflict with cancer; Gale's internal conflict with Brian's illness

Complication(s): Gale's shyness and Brian's sociability; their friendship; Gale's knee injury; Brian's illness

Climax: When Gale receives the Most Courageous Player award and dedicates it to Brian

Resolution: When Brian dies, after he and Gale have become devoted friends; Gale overcomes his shyness because of Brian's illness and friendship.

Collection Four   We Rookies Have to Stick Together

BRIAN'S SONG, PUPIL'S EDITION PAGE 274
William Blinn

Discovering Elements of Drama

A dramatic work is a story to be acted for an audience. In a dramatic work, **characters,** which may be people or animals, take part in the play's action. A **protagonist** is the play's main character; an **antagonist** is a character or situation that presents the protagonist with a **conflict,** which is a struggle or clash. **Complications** arise as the characters attempt to resolve the conflict. The **climax,** the story's turning point, is the moment of the story's highest emotional intensity, when the outcome of the conflict is revealed. During the **resolution,** the complications of the plot are finally worked out, happily or not.

Understanding Elements of Drama

On the line provided, identify each of the following aspects of *Brian's Song* as one of the elements named above. (You won't necessarily use all the elements.)

_____ **1.** Brian, when he gives Gale incorrect information about Halas

_____ **2.** Brian and Gale's individual professional hopes

_____ **3.** Brian's and Gale's becoming roommates

_____ **4.** Brian, when he is hospitalized

_____ **5.** Gale's speech to the team in the locker room

Applying Skills

6. Not every drama has a clear-cut protagonist and antagonist. Characters can switch back and forth between the roles, and other forces can become antagonistic, too. In what ways are Brian and Gale both protagonists and antagonists? What other antagonists are in the play? Write your response on the lines below.

_____

_____

_____

_____

_____

IDENTIFYING SOUND DEVICES IN A POEM   THE HIGHWAYMAN

TEACHING NOTES

This material is designed to be used with "The Highwayman" (Pupil's Edition, page 341) and the feature Elements of Literature: Poetry: Sound Effects (Pupil's Edition, page 338) in Collection Five. In this lesson, students will identify and use poetic sound devices.

Presentation

1. After students have read the selection and the Elements of Literature feature, place the Identifying Sound Devices in a Poem transparency on the overhead projector. Read and explain the definitions and examples aloud and answer any questions students have.

2. Use the following activities to help students understand and use the sound devices:
   - Clap out the rhythmic pattern of the poem's first three lines. To help students hear the beat more clearly, pause briefly after clapping each stressed syllable. Point out the similarity of the rhythmic pattern in each line.
   - Have groups of students brainstorm to come up with as many words as possible that show onomatopoeia. *Possible responses are buzz, rustle, boom, tick-tock, tweet, bark, warble, hum, whir, and meow.*
   - Ask students to think of popular songs that contain rhyme and to recite some of the lyrics.
   - Ask students if they have ever tried to say a tongue twister. Point out that alliteration is an important part of these clever sentences. For instance, "She sells seashells by the seashore" is hard to say because it repeats consonant sounds in words that are close together. Ask students if they can think of any other tongue twisters. *Another example is: "Peter Piper picked a peck of pickled peppers."*

3. Once students feel comfortable identifying and using these sound devices, have them form four groups. Assign each group a different sound device to identify in "The Highwayman." Following the transparency format, ask each group to find several examples of the sound device in the poem and to write them down. When the groups have finished, have a representative from each group come up to the overhead projector, one at a time, to write

down one or two examples in the appropriate block. Have each representative explain how the lines they write down are sound devices.

4. Ask students what effect the sound devices have in the poem. *Answers will vary. The sound devices add precise, colorful, and unique language to the poem. They add interest, excitement, and tension.*

Further Practice

For further practice on sound devices in "The Highwayman," give students the worksheet on page 16.

Alternative Uses of the Transparency

You can use the transparency with other poems. You can also use these materials with poetry-writing activities.

TRANSPARENCY ANSWER KEY

Rhythm

"And he tapped with his whip on the shutters, but all was locked and barred.
He whistled a tune to the window, and who should be waiting there" (lines 13–14)

Rhyme

Lines 1 and 2: trees / seas

Lines 7 and 8: chin / skin

Lines 49 and 50: jest / breast

Lines 75 and 78: breath / death

Onomatopoeia

Line 13: clattered, clashed

Line 14: tapped

Lines 67, 68, and 73: tlot-tlot

Line 97: clatters, clangs

Line 98: taps

Alliteration

Line 2: "**g**hostly **g**alleon"

Line 8: "**c**oat of the **c**laret," "**b**reeches of **b**rown"

Line 13: "Over the **c**obbles he **c**lattered and **c**lashed"

Line 57: "**str**etched and **str**ained"

Line 65: "**B**lank and **b**are"

Line 89: "**D**own like a **d**og"

Collection Five   Living in the Heart

THE HIGHWAYMAN, PUPIL'S EDITION PAGE 341
Alfred Noyes

Discovering Sound Devices in a Poem

Poets use various devices to enhance the sound of their work. **Rhythm** is the rise and fall of the human voice. **Rhyme** is the use of words that sound similar (such as "moon" and "tune"). **Onomatopoeia** is the use of words that sound like their meanings (such as "meow"). **Alliteration** is the placing of words that contain the same consonant sounds near each other.

Understanding Sound Devices in a Poem

On the line provided, identify at least one sound device—rhythm, rhyme, onomatopoeia, or alliteration—used in each of these passages from "The Highwayman."

_____ **1.** "Over the cobbles he clattered and clashed . . ." (line 12)

_____ **2.** "They fitted with never a wrinkle. His boots were up to the thigh." (line 9)

_____ **3.** "And dark in the dark old inn yard a stable wicket creaked / Where Tim the ostler listened. His face was white and peaked." (lines 19–20)

_____ **4.** "*Tlot-tlot; tlot-tlot!*" (line 68)

Applying Skills

5. Without sound devices a poem could end up being a story or fable. What would "The Highwayman" be without its rhythm and rhyme? On the lines below, retell "The Highwayman" without a rhyme scheme and without breaking up the lines. What has it become? Why? Would anyone want to recite it over and over?

_____

_____

_____

_____

_____

_____

_____

IDENTIFYING IMAGERY   ## ANNABEL LEE

TEACHING NOTES

This material is designed to be used with "Annabel Lee" (Pupil's Edition, page 351) and the feature Elements of Literature: Poetry: Images (Pupil's Edition, page 355) in Collection Five. In this lesson, students will identify imagery in the poem.

Presentation

1. After students have read the selection and the Elements of Literature feature, use the following activity to help students learn the function of imagery in poetry and other writing.

    Have students choose from several small objects you have brought from home or already have in the classroom. Tell them to look at their object closely and touch it, noticing how it feels in their hands. Ask them to listen to the sound it makes when they tap it or move it around, and to see if it has an aroma. Have students jot down their observations. Then, tell them to freewrite short paragraphs in which they describe their objects without naming them. When students have finished writing, have volunteers read their paragraphs aloud. Tell the rest of the class to try to guess what each object is. Explain that a description that effectively uses imagery enables the audience to identify the object described without seeing it.

2. Project the transparency Identifying Imagery and have students give examples of each kind of imagery from the paragraphs they wrote. Then, read aloud "Annabel Lee." Have students identify sensory images in the poem as you write one or two of them on the transparency. Ask students what effect the imagery has on them as they read the poem.

3. Have students read aloud some examples of images from the poem that were not mentioned in the earlier discussion. Tell them to withhold the names of the senses appealed to by the images they cite. Have the class identify the sense to which each image appeals.

4. To extend the discussion, ask students to respond to the following item: Describe the feelings you had when reading "Annabel Lee." Do you think you would feel differently about the poem if it did not contain images that appeal to the senses? Explain your answer. *Students may feel sadness, fear, or nostalgia*

when reading "Annabel Lee." Some students might say they would feel differently about the poem if it did not contain images appealing to the senses. These images are vivid and may evoke strong feelings in the reader.

5. Although a feeling of loss may be painful, it can also help people grow and learn more about the human condition. Explain to students that a feeling of loss can have many causes. A feeling of loss may result from a move to another city or town or from the disappearance of a treasured object. As an additional activity, you may wish to have students write poems about losses in their lives that they feel comfortable sharing. Have them use imagery to convey their feelings. Students who do not wish to write about loss might write about people, places, or things that they value.

Further Practice

For further practice on imagery in "Annabel Lee," give students the worksheet on page 19.

Alternative Uses of the Transparency

Give students copies of the transparency to use before they begin writing original poems or stories. You can also use the transparency when students analyze other poems or short stories.

TRANSPARENCY ANSWER KEY

Sense of sight

"In a kingdom by the sea" (line 2)

"her highborn kinsmen came / And bore her away" (lines 17–18)

"To shut her up in a sepulcher" (line 19)

"wingèd seraphs" (line 11)

"For the moon never beams" (line 34)

"And the stars never rise" (line 36)

Sense of hearing

"by the sounding sea" (line 41)

Sense of touch

"A wind blew out of a cloud" (line 15)

"chilling / My beautiful Annabel Lee" (lines 15–16)

"Chilling and killing my Annabel Lee" (line 26)

"but I feel the bright eyes" (line 36)

ELEMENTS OF LITERATURE   FIRST COURSE   **LITERARY ELEMENTS**

Collection Five   Living in the Heart   WORKSHEET **6**

ANNABEL LEE, PUPIL'S EDITION PAGE 351
Edgar Allan Poe

Discovering Imagery

Poets use **imagery** to give the reader a physical sense of the poem's subject. Imagery can appeal to the reader's sense of sight, hearing, touch, or smell. Its effect is often to convey a feeling or mood.

Understanding Imagery

On the lines provided, state in your own words what each of the following phrases from "Annabel Lee" is describing. Then, identify the sense or senses to which the imagery appeals.

1. "*I* was a child and *she* was a child . . ." (line 7)

_____

_____

2. " . . . the wingèd seraphs of heaven . . ." (line 11)

_____

_____

3. "A wind blew out of a cloud, chilling / My beautiful Annabel Lee." (lines 15–16)

_____

_____

4. "In her tomb by the sounding sea." (line 41)

_____

_____

Applying Skills

5. Although many of the images in "Annabel Lee" are of the seaside, there is also a great deal of imagery about the sky. On a separate sheet of paper, identify the images of the sky and heaven in the poem. How would you describe the mood these images create?

IDENTIFYING FIGURES OF SPEECH

MY FATHER IS A SIMPLE MAN

TEACHING NOTES

This material is designed to be used with "My Father Is a Simple Man" (Pupil's Edition, page 399) and the feature Elements of Literature: Poetry: Figures of Speech (Pupil's Edition, page 397) in Collection Five. In this lesson, students will identify and create similes, metaphors, and personifications.

Presentation

1. After students have read the selection and the Elements of Literature feature, place the Identifying Figures of Speech transparency on the overhead projector. Have volunteers read the definitions and examples aloud. Ask students if they can think of other examples of the three figures of speech.

2. You may use the following activities to continue the presentation of figures of speech:
    *   Have students quickly jot down the names of ten inanimate objects. Have partners share their lists and write personifications for five of the objects on their combined lists.
    *   Read the following sentences aloud to the class. Ask them to identify the metaphors and to tell what they refer to.
        a. The wheat field was a sea of gold.
        b. Talisha is my little sister.
        c. Grandpa's reply was music to my ears.
        d. The evening star is a diamond of light.
        e. Toby is such a pack rat!
        f. The wheat field is golden.
        Sentences **a, c, d,** and **e** contain metaphors. Sentence **(a)** compares a field with a sea, **(c)** a reply with music, **(d)** the evening star with a diamond, and **(e)** Toby with a pack rat.

3. Give students copies of the transparency on which they will identify the figures of speech in "My Father Is a Simple Man." Ask the following questions to help students understand the significance of the poem's figures of speech:
    *   Poets often use similes to give the reader a clearer insight into the meaning of the poem's theme. What insights do the two similes in this poem give you? *Answers will vary. The simile "like the orange trees" means that we all participate in the perpetual return of life. The simile "like a punishing/evil stranger" means that harsh things are unavoidable aspects of life.*

*   "He has taken me on this journey/and it's been lifelong" is a metaphor from the poem. This metaphor compares life to a walk to town. What are some ways in which life is like a journey? *Answers will vary. Life is like a journey because both begin in one place, are filled with events, and end in another place.*

4. As an extension activity, have students write a simile, metaphor, or personification comparing an emotion, such as love or hope, to something else. Have students exchange papers and identify their partner's figures of speech as metaphors, similes, or personifications.

Further Practice

For further practice on figures of speech in "My Father Is a Simple Man," give students the worksheet on page 22.

Alternative Uses of the Transparency

Students can use copies of the transparency with poetry-writing activities. You can also use the transparency when students analyze any other poem.

TRANSPARENCY ANSWER KEY

Simile

Lines 14–15: "and we too will come back
like the orange trees."

Lines 26–28: "and when the bitter-hard reality
comes at me like a punishing
evil stranger"

Metaphor

Line 7:   "it is the fruit of scholars."

Lines 8–9: "He has taken me on this journey
and it's been lifelong." (extended
metaphor)

Line 25:   "he's the scholar"

Personification: none

From "My Father Is a Simple Man" from *The Sadness of Days: Selected and New Poems* by Luis Omar Salinas. Copyright © 1987 by Luis Omar Salinas. Published by **Arte Público Press**-University of Houston, Houston, TX, 1987. Reprinted by permission of the publisher.

|

Collection Five   Living in the Heart |

MY FATHER IS A SIMPLE MAN, PUPIL'S EDITION PAGE 399
Luis Omar Salinas

Discovering Figures of Speech

Figures of speech are expressions that illustrate a meaning through a comparison or some other statement that isn't literally true. They include **similes,** expressions that compare two unlike things by using *like* or *as,* and **metaphors,** in which one thing is said to *be* another thing. A metaphor does not use *like* or *as*. **Personification** is a technique in which a nonhuman thing or quality is discussed as if it were human.

Understanding Figures of Speech

For each of the figures of speech below from "My Father Is a Simple Man," state whether it is a simile, metaphor, or personification. Then, explain what the comparison means. (You may need to refer to the whole poem to know a comparison's meaning.) Write your response on the lines provided. Examples may include more than one figure of speech.

1. "and we too will come back / like the orange trees." (lines 14–15)

   _____

2. "The truth of it is, he's the scholar . . ." (line 25)

   _____

3. "the bitter-hard reality / comes at me like a punishing / evil stranger . . ." (lines 26–28)

   _____

4. "I convince / him it is the fruit of scholars."(lines 6–7)

   _____

Applying Skills

5. The sentence "I ask him what he thinks / about death and he says / he will gladly face it when / it comes but won't jump / out in front of a car" is not meant completely literally. What does the father mean when he tells his thoughts on death? Write your response on a separate sheet of paper.

From "My Father Is a Simple Man" from *The Sadness of Days: Selected and New Poems* by Luis Omar Salinas. Copyright © 1987 by Luis Omar Salinas. Published by **Arte Público Press**-University of Houston, Houston, TX, 1987. Reprinted by permission of the publisher.

NONFICTION: INFERRING THE MAIN IDEA

WHEN THE EARTH SHAKES

TEACHING NOTES

This material is designed to be used with "When the Earth Shakes" (Pupil's Edition, page 435) and the feature Elements of Literature: Nonfiction: The Main Idea (Pupil's Edition, page 443) in Collection Six. In this lesson, students will infer the main idea in the selection.

Presentation

1. After students have read the selection and the Elements of Literature feature, begin the lesson by asking them to look up the words *infer* and *imply* in a dictionary. The following questions will guide the discussion:
   - What does the word *imply* mean? *To suggest, to hint at, or to say indirectly.*
   - What does the word *infer* mean? *To decide or draw a conclusion on the basis of evidence.*
   - Inferring, or drawing a conclusion from information that is implied, is like solving a mystery from clues. Pretend you overheard the following conversation:

   Jay: "That was a waste of time."
   Tiffany: "It wasn't so bad. And the popcorn was good."
   Jay: "Well, I'd rather see some action with Stallone or Schwarzenegger."
   Tiffany: "You're definitely not a romantic."

   Using your detective skills, what information can you infer from the conversation? *Students may infer that Jay and Tiffany saw a movie together, that they saw the movie at a theater, that they ate popcorn, that Jay did not like the movie, that the movie was a romance instead of an action movie, and that Tiffany enjoyed the movie.*

2. Place the Nonfiction: Inferring the Main Idea transparency on the overhead projector. Have students suggest responses to the questions as you write them on the transparency.

3. To extend the discussion, ask students why the author devotes so much attention to scientific information related to the cause of earthquakes. You might explain to students that the information supports the description of the destruction caused by the Alaskan earthquake in 1964.

Further Practice

For further practice on main idea in "When the Earth Shakes," give students the worksheet on page 25.

Alternative Uses of the Transparency

You can use the transparency with other nonfiction essays to remind students to use details to infer the main idea.

TRANSPARENCY ANSWER KEY

1. The 1964 Alaskan earthquake.

2. Possible responses: Structures broke apart during the earthquake. The earthquake caused fires from oil tanks. The earthquake was the result of rocks shifting and splitting.

3. Shifting rocks in the earth caused massive damage in Alaska.

4. Yes. Possible response: "During that time, the earthquake did great damage."

5. Possible response: The shifting of rocks in the earth resulted in terrible destruction in Alaska in 1964.

|

Collection Six   This Old Earth |

WHEN THE EARTH SHAKES, PUPIL'S EDITION PAGE 435
Patricia Lauber

Discovering the Main Idea

A paragraph's **topic** is its subject—what the piece of writing is about. The most important idea expressed about the topic is its **main idea.** A main idea is supported by **details** in the paragraph. A writer may state the main idea of a story directly; however, a reader may have to make an **inference,** or educated guess, by examining the evidence provided by the writer.

Understanding the Main Idea

For each of the following details, infer from it what you can about its larger meaning. Write your inferences on the lines provided.

1. "Suddenly the familiar and the cozy vanished. In their place came the strange and the fearful." (page 436)

   _____

2. "By 5:38 half of Alaska seemed to be in the grip of an angry giant." (page 436)

   _____

3. "Much of Alaska's coast is rugged, rocky land that stands high above the water. The port towns were built in the low-lying places. But here the ground was not very solid." (page 436)

   _____

4. "When the quake ended, the town of Valdez was ten feet higher than it had been before." (page 437)

   _____

Applying Skills

5. "When the Earth Shakes" begins with a description of a town at a quiet moment on a Friday afternoon. This peaceful scene is quickly followed by descriptions of a huge disaster. Why do you think the author chose to start this way, rather than state her main idea right away? Write your response on a separate sheet of paper.

From "When the Earth Shakes" from *Earthquakes: New Scientific Ideas About How and Why the Earth Shakes* by Patricia Lauber. Copyright © 1972 by **Patricia Lauber.** Reprinted by permission of the author.

WORDS FROM MYTHOLOGY

TEACHING NOTES

This material is designed to be used with Greek and Roman myths (Pupil's Edition, pages 501–561) and with the feature Elements of Literature: The Myths of Greece and Rome (Pupil's Edition, page 496) in Collection Seven. In this lesson, students will define and trace the origins of words from myths.

Presentation

1. After students have read the selections and the Elements of Literature feature, begin the presentation by drawing on students' prior knowledge of words assimilated into English from other languages. To begin the discussion, you may wish to ask the following questions:
   - Can you think of words from the Spanish language that we use in English? *Possible responses: barbecue, rodeo, avocado, alligator, potato, tortilla, frijoles, patio, pinto, stampede, and tornado.*
   - From what other languages have we borrowed words? *Students might say French, Italian, German, and the American Indian languages.*
     Tell students that we also use words that came from classical Greek and Latin and that some of these words came from myths.

2. Place the Words from Mythology transparency on the overhead projector. Have students work individually using a dictionary to define each word on the chart. Ask volunteers to read their definitions as you write them on the transparency. Next, ask students to identify the name from mythology that is similar to each word and to describe the related mythological character as you write the names and descriptions on the transparency.

3. To extend the lesson, ask students to use words from the chart when writing their own myths. Possible topics include explanations of natural occurrences such as tornados, droughts, snow, hail, or earthquakes. Students may pattern their stories after "The Origin of the Seasons" (Pupil's Edition, page 501) or create their own struc-

THE MYTHS OF GREECE AND ROME

tures. You might encourage them to imagine what it would be like to experience a tornado or an earthquake without knowing the scientific explanation for the occurrence. Have volunteers read their myths aloud in class.

Further Practice

For further practice on mythology, give students the worksheet on page 28.

Alternative Uses of the Transparency

Students can use copies of the transparency when they study the myths in Collection Seven.

TRANSPARENCY ANSWER KEY

helium: a gas used to inflate balloons / Helios / god of the sun

nemesis: one who avenges relentlessly / Nemesis / goddess of retribution who made sure all evil and all good were rewarded

iris: part of the eye; a flower / Iris / rainbow goddess; messenger of the gods

echo: repetition of sound / Echo / nymph who fell in love with Narcissus

narcissistic: vain, egotistical / Narcissus / mortal who fell in love with his reflection

jovial: jolly, merry / Jove or Jupiter (Roman name for Zeus) / leader of gods

muse: ponder, think about / Muses / goddesses of the arts and sciences

panic: sudden fear / Pan / god of nature

martial: warlike / Mars (Ares) / god of war

cereal: breakfast food such as cornflakes or oatmeal / Ceres (Demeter) / goddess of the harvest

vulcanize: process of hardening and strengthening rubber / Vulcan (Hephaestus) / god of smiths and fire

Olympics: international games held every four years / Olympus / highest mountain in Greece; home of the gods

ELEMENTS OF LITERATURE   FIRST COURSE   **LITERARY ELEMENTS**

Collection Seven   Our Classical Heritage   **WORKSHEET 9**

THE MYTHS OF GREECE AND ROME, PUPIL'S EDITION PAGES 501–561

Discovering Mythology

Every culture has some kind of mythology, a set of stories that were created in early times to help people explain and understand their lives and the world around them.

Understanding Mythology

The myths of ancient Greece and Rome often feature characters whose behavior is flawed. Their flaws and weaknesses are familiar and understandable to us because they are human. For each of the mythological characters below, identify the flaw or weakness the character exhibits at the moment described, and explain the consequences of the flaw. Write your response on the lines provided.

1. Orpheus, on his way back from the underworld

_____

_____

2. Narcissus, when he encounters a pond

_____

_____

3. Icarus, while escaping the island

_____

_____

4. Midas, when asking Dionysus for a gift

_____

_____

Applying Skills

5. The gods and goddesses in these myths are not always above human flaws, such as jealousy, spite, etc. Hera is jealous when Zeus flirts with nymphs, and when Demeter is grieving, she spreads her misery to others. What conclusions can you draw from this about the Greek and Roman idea of what a god or goddess would be like? Explain your answer. Write your response on a separate sheet of paper.

FABLES: A MISHAP LEADS TO A LESSON

AESOP'S FABLES

TEACHING NOTES

This material is designed to be used with Aesop's Fables (Pupil's Edition, pages 567–572) and with the feature Elements of Literature: Fables: Teaching Stories (Pupil's Edition page 565). In this lesson, students will analyze and compare the lessons in each of four fables.

Presentation

1. After students have read the selections and the Elements of Literature feature, place the Fables: A Mishap Leads to a Lesson transparency on the overhead projector. Open the discussion by having students talk about the meanings of the following sayings.
   - Don't cry over spilled milk.
   - Don't put all your eggs in one basket.
   - The squeakiest wheel gets the oil.
   - What goes around comes around.

2. Discuss with students the way fables illustrate nuggets of wisdom. Often, in a fable, something goes wrong and sheds light on some truth about life. Ask students to think of fable-like things that happen in real life, such as the following situations.
   - *A student makes fun of someone else, then trips over his or her own shoelaces.*
   - *The owners of a company get overconfident and stop listening to customers, and their new product fails.*
   - *A greedy person hoards money but never manages to enjoy it during his or her lifetime.*

3. Ask students what fables, or other stories with morals, they have heard in real life, perhaps from their parents or other adults. What have their parents (or others) used the fables for? A couple of examples include the tale of the hen who wouldn't share her bread with the other animals because they wouldn't help her make it, and the tale of the tortoise and the hare, in which slow, steady effort triumphs over careless speed. Students' tales may come from all different traditions. Some may simply be made up. What they should have in common is that they have a moral or lesson at the end.

4. As a class, have students fill in the chart with the mishap or conflict that takes place in each fable in the pupil's edition, followed by the outcome, followed by the lesson that the fable teaches. Discuss each fable as the chart is filled in.

5. As an extension activity, have students compare the lessons in the fables with the lessons in Greek and Roman myths. Ask them to discuss what fables and myths have in common, and what universal human concerns they can draw from these readings. Have them write an essay about these similarities.

Further Practice

For further practice on fables, give students the worksheet on page 31.

Alternative Uses of the Transparency

Students can use copies of the transparency with a collection of fables, such as *Aesop's Fables,* substituting new fable titles.

TRANSPARENCY ANSWER KEY

The Frogs Who Wished for a King: *Mishap:* The frogs become lazy and ask for a government that will entertain them. *Outcome:* They get a cruel king. *Lesson:* Before you try to change your situation, make sure you can improve it.

The Fox and the Grapes: *Mishap:* The fox can't reach the grapes. *Outcome:* He goes off, claiming they are sour. *Lesson:* Those who fail and claim that the prize wasn't so great are just pretending they don't care about their failure.

The Town Mouse and the Country Mouse: *Mishap:* The town mouse belittles the country mouse's simple ways. Both mice go to town to feast and are almost killed by cats and people. *Outcome:* The country mouse tells the town mouse that she prefers the simple country, without urban dangers. *Lesson:* It's better to live a poor, secure life than a wealthy, dangerous one.

Belling the Cat: *Mishap:* The mice live in terror of the cat and decide to put a bell on it. *Outcome:* No one will bell the cat. *Lesson:* Many things are more easily said than done.

AESOP'S FABLES, PUPIL'S EDITION PAGES 567–572

Discovering Fables

Most fables teach moral lessons and illustrate the ways people behave. They are usually very short stories, often with animals as characters, with a moral given at the end.

Understanding Fables

On the lines provided, describe the human behavior illustrated by the following situations from the fables.

1. The fox stalks away from the grapevine, complaining that the grapes are sour anyway.

_____

_____

2. The neighbors fail to respond to the shepherd boy's real cry for help.

_____

_____

3. The mice decide to put a bell on the cat but fail to execute their plan.

_____

_____

4. The Town Mouse looks down on the Country Mouse's ways.

_____

_____

Applying Skills

5. On a separate sheet of paper, explain the meanings and origins of the phrases "sour grapes" and "never cry wolf," using what you have learned from these fables.

Collection Eight   900 Cinderellas

FOLK TALES: IDENTIFYING CHARACTER TYPES   FOLK TALES

TEACHING NOTES

This material is designed to be used with the folk tales (Pupil's Edition pages 593–665) and with the feature Elements of Literature: Folk Tales: Telling Tales (Pupil's Edition, page 625) in Collection Eight. In this lesson, students will identify, compare, and contrast six character types in four folk tales.

Presentation

1. After students have read the selections and the Elements of Literature feature, place the Folk Tales: Identifying Character Types transparency on the overhead projector. Begin the discussion of character types by asking students to name some familiar folk tale characters. *The wicked stepmother and the cruel stepsisters are vain and proud characters who mistreat the main character. The handsome royal character ultimately saves the main character from her miserable life. The animal helps and supports the main character by providing a refuge, an escape for the main character, and usually a means to overcome hardship. The father is usually kind, sometimes rich, but often oblivious to what is happening.*

2. As a means of review, ask volunteers to summarize each of the four folk tales listed on the chart. Next, have students identify the different character types from each folk tale as you fill in the appropriate boxes on the chart. Every character type may not appear in each folk tale.

3. To extend the discussion of character types, ask students the following questions:
   • Why does the kind character always seem to be an outsider? *Aside from the father, the rest of the family members are cruel and wicked. Therefore, since the family is of no help, there is a need for an outside character who is helpful and kind.*
   • Why do you think there is usually at least one stepsister in addition to the wicked stepmother? Why is there usually a stepmother and stepsister(s) instead of mother and sisters? *They play off each other and often gang up on the main character. Sometimes one of the sisters is kinder than the other.*
   • In general, is there usually a happy ending for the main character in most folk tales? Why or

why not? *Generally, there is a happy ending, and the folk tale usually teaches a lesson or moral.*

Further Practice

For futher practice on folk tales, give students the worksheet on page 34.

Alternative Uses of the Transparency

By changing the story titles, the transparency can be used to compare the characters in other folk tales.

TRANSPARENCY ANSWER KEY

ASCHENPUTTEL

Wicked Stepmother: Yes
Cruel Stepsisters: Yes
Royal Character: Prince
Animal: Various birds
Kind Characters: No
Father: Yes—a rich man

THE ALGONQUIN CINDERELLA

Wicked Stepmother: No
Cruel Stepsisters: Yes—one
Royal Character: Not royal—the Invisible One
Animal: No
Kind Characters: The second sister and the Invisible One's sister
Father: Yes—a widower

YEH-SHEN

Wicked Stepmother: Yes
Cruel Stepsisters: Yes—one
Royal Character: A king
Animal: Fish
Kind Characters: An old man
Father: No—Chief Wu

ASHPET

Wicked Stepmother: No—a wicked employer
Cruel Stepsisters: No—the employer's two daughters
Royal Character: No
Animal: No
Kind Characters: An old woman
Father: No

Collection Eight   900 Cinderellas

FOLK TALES, PUPIL'S EDITION PAGES 593–665

Discovering Folk Tales

Folk tales are handed down in every culture, sometimes in writing, but often orally. Sometimes they change slightly over the years, but they usually retain a moral or lesson about life. Certain folk tales occur, with changes in details, in several different traditions.

Understanding Folk Tales

On the lines provided, write what human quality each of these folk tale characters represents. Then, explain what lesson about life the character's experiences teach.

1. from "Oni and the Great Bird," the impostor who claims he is the one who killed Anodo

_____

_____

2. from "Master Frog," the youngest daughter, Kien Tien, who agrees to marry the frog

_____

_____

3. from "The Hummingbird King," Chirumá, the uncle of Kukul

_____

_____

4. from the three different "Cinderella" tales, the girl who is mistreated by her sisters or stepsisters

_____

_____

Applying Skills

5. The seal in "Sealskin, Soulskin" and the bird in "The Hummingbird King" both have special ties to human communities. Why do you think storytellers felt the need to connect these animals to people? On a separate sheet of paper, describe the special ties between humans and animals in these stories, and discuss why you think this special bond is depicted.

Rikki-tikki-tavi, page 4

Understanding Elements of a Short Story

1. The main conflict is between the cobras and the other residents of the garden (birds, Rikki, people) who wish to possess it.
2. Nagaina's attempt to avenge her husband's death
3. The battle between Rikki and Nagaina.
4. Rikki continues to watch over the garden and protect the family.

Applying Skills

(Responses will vary. Two sample responses follow.)
5. Rikki-tikki may be seen as a hero because he acts to protect the helpless birds and the humans, including a little boy. The cobras may appear vicious and cruel and deserving of their fate.

   On the other hand, Rikki-tikki may be seen as selfishly trying to win the favor of the humans so that he can stuff himself at their dinner table and live in comfort. He kills the cobras, who are only trying to raise a family, and destroys their eggs. The story can be validly viewed as a struggle for survival in a limited space, where no creature's interests are superior to another's.

from Homesick, page 7

Understanding Tone in Nonfiction

1. subjective
2. objective
3. objective
4. subjective

Applying Skills

(Responses will vary. A sample response follows.)
5. The final two actions show that the narrator is happy and secure with her identity as an American. The narrator's correction of her false English lesson shows that she does respect and care about Lin Nai-Nai, and her facing up to Ian Forbes shows that she has found a way to be American even when "doing as the Romans do."

After Twenty Years, page 10

Understanding Point of View in a Story

1. Omniscient
2. The narrator does not reveal that the policeman is Jimmy.
3. The fact that this man is not Jimmy is withheld.
4. If the story were told from third-person limited or first-person perspective, it would have been colored by the feelings, interests, and personalities of the character who was telling the story.

Applying Skills

(Responses will vary. A sample response follows.)
5. Ending the story with the note from Jimmy and no description of Bob's feelings allows the reader to experience the very chill of recognition that is creeping up Bob's spine as he reads the note. Revealing Bob's thoughts during the story would have taken away the reader's surprise at finding out, all at once, that (1) Bob is a wanted criminal, (2) the policeman is Jimmy himself, and (3) Bob's criminal career is over.

Brian's Song, page 13

Understanding Elements of Drama

1. antagonist
2. conflict
3. complication
4. protagonist
5. climax

Applying Skills

(Responses will vary. A sample response follows.)
6. Brian and Gale are both protagonists in their struggles to succeed in professional football, and in their struggles to understand life's difficulties. They become each other's antagonists when they have to compete for the same position. Other antagonists are Gale's injury, Brian's illness, and the professional sports system, which rewards performance and ignores individual tragedies.

The Highwayman, page 16

Understanding Sound Devices in a Poem

1. alliteration
2. rhythm
3. rhyme
4. onomatopoeia

Applying Skills

(Responses will vary. A sample response follows.)
5. A girl, daughter of an innkeeper, sees off her sweetheart, a robber who promises to return to her that night. The next day, when he still has not returned, a band of armed men take over the inn. They tie the girl up with a gun pointing to her chest so she cannot escape. She can see the road, though, and manages to get a finger on the trigger. When she sees her sweetheart returning, she fires the gun, saving his life but ending

hers. Later, when the robber finds out what has happened to his true love, he storms up to the inn and is immediately shot. According to legend, the ghosts of the two lovers still meet on some nights.

The poem has become a story. There is nothing poetic about it anymore. It does not invite repetition or re-reading, as the poem does.

Annabel Lee, page 19

Understanding Imagery

1. The image is of a young girl and a young boy, even if Poe does not mean this literally. The sense is of sight.
2. The image is of angels, perhaps floating on their wings. The sense is of sight.
3. The image is of a windy day, with a young woman who is catching a chill from the cold. The senses are of sight, touch, and possibly even hearing (the sound of wind).
4. The image is of a grave near the ocean, probably with waves crashing. The senses are of sight and hearing.

Applying Skills

(Responses will vary. A sample response follows.)
5. Images include: "the wingèd seraphs of heaven," "A wind blew out of a cloud," "The angels, not half so happy in heaven," "the wind came out of the cloud by night," "the angels in heaven above," "the moon never beams," and "the stars never rise."

The images create a sense of helplessness on the part of the people. The angels, stars, and moon all look down on them, and the angels are cruel to them. The stars and moon are indifferent to them. The mood is somber and mournful, yet hopeful.

My Father Is a Simple Man, page 22

Understanding Figures of Speech

1. Simile. People are also always dying and being born, in the same way that orange trees are.
2. Metaphor. The father is not literally a scholar, but he is wiser than his son in the ways of life.
3. Simile. Life can produce cruel surprises, just like a person on the street who does something bad to you.
Personification. Reality is described as if it were a living thing, a threatening stranger.

4. Metaphor. The pomegranate is really just another fruit, but the son is saying that it has special significance to educated people.

Applying Skills

(Responses will vary. A sample response follows.)
5. The father means that although he accepts that death cannot be avoided, he is still going to live in a way that does not invite death to come earlier. He knows death is coming, but he is not afraid to love life.

When the Earth Shakes, page 25

Understanding the Main Idea

1. Something terrible happened.
2. Alaska was hit by a major natural disaster.
3. This location suffered unusually severe damage because the ground was not particularly solid.
4. The shifting that causes earthquakes can change the altitudes of whole towns.

Applying Skills

(Responses will vary. A sample response follows.)
5. The opening scene grabs the reader's attention by showing how the disaster struck an ordinary town on an ordinary day. It begins like a movie or a novel, rather than as a nonfiction article about the science of earthquakes. The effect is to seize and hold the reader's interest, and help the reader understand the importance of the scientific facts.

The Myths of Greece and Rome, page 28

Understanding Mythology

1. Lack of faith or confidence. As a result, Orpheus breaks his agreement with the king of the underworld and loses Eurydice.
2. Vanity. Narcissus is doomed to love someone who does not exist (a reflection of his face in the pond).
3. Carelessness or overexcitement; ignoring his father's warnings. Icarus flies too high and the wax holding the feathers on his wings melts; he falls into the sea to his death.
4. Greed. Midas's golden touch makes him unable to eat or drink and causes him to repent of his choice. Before he can act on his change of heart, his daughter turns to gold, too, causing him grief and intensifying his repentance.

Applying Skills

(Responses will vary. A sample response follows.)

5. The ancient Greeks and Romans did not imagine that gods and goddesses were always morally superior to people. To them, deities were like humans, only with greater powers and immortality. Their actions, like the actions of mortals in these myths, shed light on human behavior.

Aesop's Fables, page 31

Understanding Fables

1. The bitterness of failure. The fox pretends he didn't want the grapes, anyway, just as a person who fails to achieve something may pretend he/she never wanted to reach the goal, anyway.

2. Like any group of people who have been falsely roused more than once, they have become accustomed to his false alarms.

3. Things are easier said than done. Although the idea sounded good, the task is much harder than they thought.

4. Sometimes people who are wealthier and more worldly look down on people who choose to live simpler, less luxurious lives.

Applying Skills

(Responses will vary. A sample response follows.)

5. "Sour grapes" is used to describe people who would rather cut down the things they failed to get than admit that they failed to reach their goals. The phrase refers to the story of the fox who couldn't reach the grapes and then pretended the grapes were sour.

"Never cry wolf" is a warning that means one should not raise false alarms just to get a reaction, because when one really needs help, no one will believe the warning. The phrase comes from the story of the shepherd boy who hated his job and cried "wolf" just to get a reaction from people. When a wolf actually came, they ignored his cries, and he was gobbled up.

Folk Tales, page 34

Understanding Folk Tales

1. Greed and dishonesty. The tale shows that such a liar is exposed and punished in the end.

2. Altruism and/or willingness to accept someone others do not take seriously. Since she ends up happily married to a prince, the lesson is that unselfish acceptance of someone else—and the willingness to sacrifice one's own happiness to save others—eventually is rewarded.

3. Greed and/or jealousy. The lesson is that even though a greedy and jealous person may get what he/she wants, justice eventually prevails. Chirumá becomes king, but he loses a battle and is taken prisoner by the enemy.

4. Goodness and/or purity of spirit. Each of these girls ends up outdoing her sisters in beauty and marrying happily. The lesson is that goodness triumphs.

Applying Skills

(Responses will vary. A sample response follows.)

5. The seal contains a woman, who spent several years living as a human, out of her element. The son she had with a man is still bonded to her. Storytellers may have made up this tale to explain why seals have human expressions in their eyes sometimes, and seem to interact with humans in a meaningful way. Other possible answers: the Inuit landscape is lonely for humans, who feel a bond with the animals around them; or the folk tale shows a deep-rooted respect for seals, which are an important part of Inuit life.

The bird *kukul* is the new form of Kukul the man, who fought bravely and was wronged by his jealous uncle. The tale may exist to create a symbol for a good person who is unjustly killed, and to anchor this symbol in a kind of bird, who then serves as a reminder that justice eventually is served.

ABOUT THE POETRY TRANSPARENCIES

The **Poetry Transparencies** include teaching notes and five transparencies that focus on a single poem from the Pupil's Edition. The poem itself appears on one transparency and is accompanied by four transparency overlays. The overlays offer an in-depth examination of various elements of the poem such as rhythm, rhyme, figures of speech, imagery, diction, and interpretation.

MADAM AND THE RENT MAN

TEACHING NOTES

This material may be used with "Madam and the Rent Man" (Pupil's Edition, page 227) and with the Poetry: Sound Effects feature (Pupil's Edition, page 338) in Collection Five. In this lesson, students will analyze the rhythm, rhyme and other sound effects, dialect, and meaning of the poem.

Presentation

1. Place the transparency of "Madam and the Rent Man" on the overhead projector. Read or have a volunteer read the poem aloud; then, ask students to describe the situation and the characters depicted in the poem.

2. Place the Rhythm in a Free Verse Poem transparency overlay over the poem. Have students clap out the rhythm of the poem. Then have them define the following terms: *free verse, iambic, trochaic,* and *anapestic.*

3. Remove the Rhythm in a Free Verse Poem overlay, and place the Rhyme and Other Sound Effects transparency overlay on top of the poem. Have a volunteer read aloud the lines that rhyme. You may wish to explain that, unlike this poem, many modern poems do not have traditional end rhymes, but instead may contain a limited number of rhymes that serve to emphasize particular lines. Ask students if they think that the rhyme is important to this poem and if so, in what way it is important.

4. Replace the Rhyme and Other Sound Effects overlay with the Dialect transparency overlay. Have students answer the questions on the overlay.

5. Replace the Dialect transparency with the Reading and Interpreting a Poem overlay. Have students answer the questions on the overlay. Ask them to discuss how they think each element contributes to the meaning and overall impact of the poem.

TRANSPARENCY ANSWER KEY

Dialect

- There are several examples of dialect in this [third] stanza. What are they? *Broke (broken), don't (doesn't), ain't (haven't), and to've (to have).*

- How would the third line [fourth stanza] appear in standard English? *"There are rats in the cellar."*

- "Pass the buck" is a colloquial expression. Why is it especially appropriate here? *The expression "pass the buck" means to pass responsibility onto someone else, which is one of the things Madam and the rent man are arguing about. Because the argument is also about money, the phrase is very appropriate.*

Reading and Interpreting a Poem

- What is the tone of the first part of the dialogue between Madam and the rent man? *Formal, cordial.*

- Are the characters polite or hostile toward each other? *Polite.*

- How does the tone change in this [second] stanza? *Madam expresses annoyance, anger, and determination.*

- What do the details of setting and the dialect in these [third and fourth] stanzas suggest about the place where the woman lives and about her financial status? *Everything in the woman's home is broken, leaking, or out of order. The woman is poor.*

- What do these lines [fifth stanza] indicate about the character of the rent man? *That he doesn't want to get involved in a dispute or take action on behalf of the tenant. He claims to be powerless over the situation.*

- Madam is firm with the rent man. Is she right, in your opinion? Why or why not? *Answers will vary. Students should give logical reasons and examples to support their opinions.*